Bibliographic information about the German National Library:
The German National Library lists this issue in the German National bibliography, more detailed bibliographic information can be found online at www.dnb.de (info completely in German)

©2014 Susanne Nagel
Illustrated by Catarina Herrmann
Translated by Simone Lalla-Fremont
Produced and published by BoD Books on Demand,
Norderstedt, Germany

ISBN: 978 - 3 - 7412 - 2398 - 3

This book is dedicated to my family
Klaus, Julia, Inka, Nicolas and Caspar,
who gave me enough courage and support
during further education and
examination periods.
They were the ones making this book possible.
Special thanks goes out to Stefan Collier for his
unwavering commitment to teach us German
opticians about Behavioral / Functional
Optometry and to realize that there is more to
sight than perfect 20/20 vision.

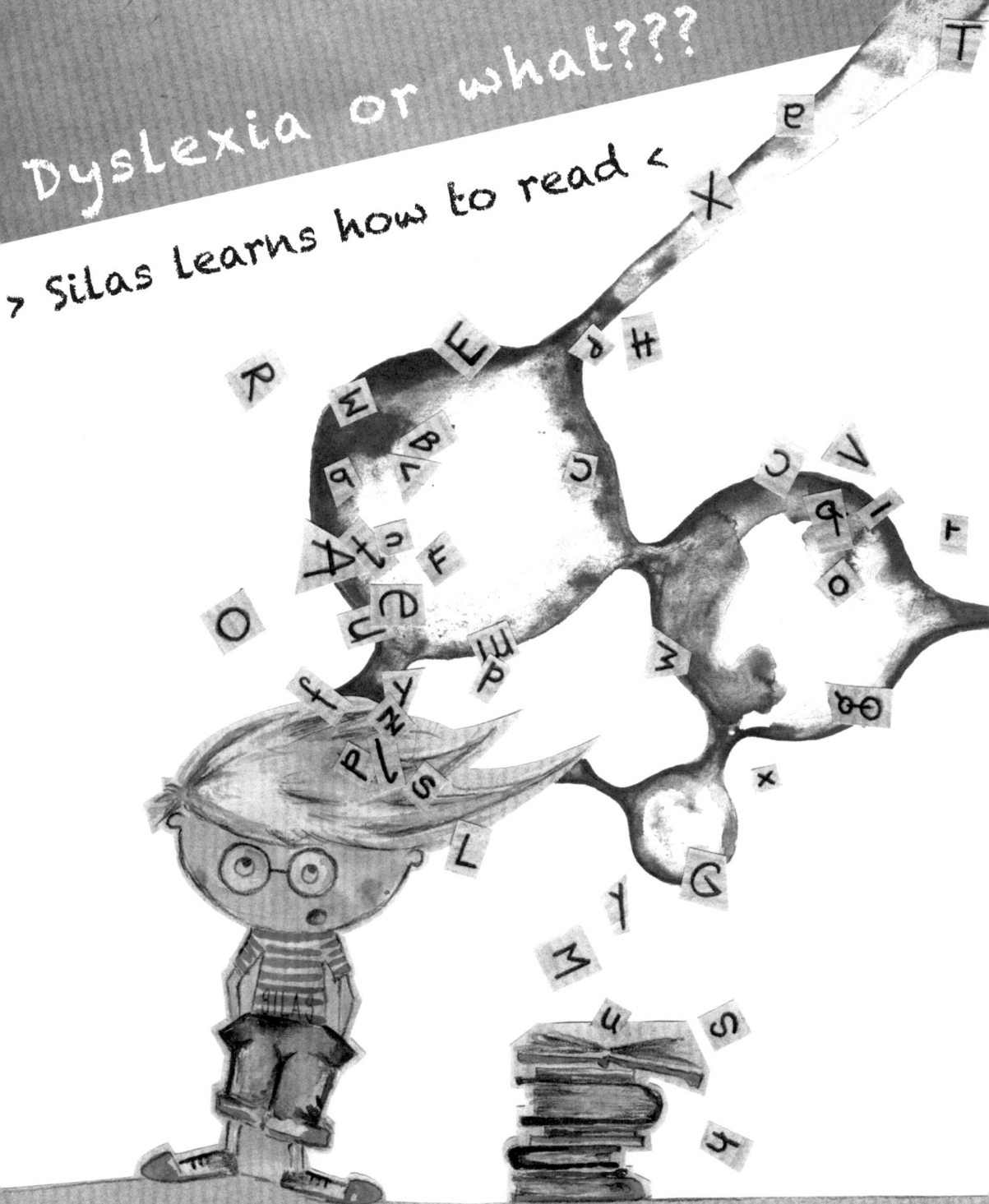

Dyslexia or what???
> Silas learns how to read <

Susanne Nagel
Optician and optometrist
illustrated by Catarina Herrmann • translated by Simone Lalla-Fremont

Contents

8–11	Chapter 1	>Silas<
12–13	Chapter 2	>Today is a good day<<
14–17	Chapter 3	>Dyslexia or what?<
18–21	Chapter 4	>Dad loses his temper<<
22–25	Chapter 5	>At the Learning Institute<
26–29	Chapter 6	>Headaches<
30–33	Chapter 7	>The last try<<
34–37	Chapter 8	>The eye exam<
38–41	Chapter 9	>Silas's eyes are like two horses<
42–43	Chapter 10	>The light shower<
44–45	Chapter 11	>Training<
46–47	Chapter 12	>Success!<

Chapter 1

> Silas <

"Silas", Mom whispers, "Silas come on you have to get up. You're going to be late for school."
"Ugh", Silas thinks and turns around.
"Is it Monday again already?"
Silas slowly gets up and walks into the bathroom with heavy feet. After getting dressed he walks downstairs where mom is waiting with his breakfast.
"Hey there big guy, did you have a good night?", she asks while pouring milk over his cereal. "Hmmmm", Silas grumbles and halfheartedly stirs in his bowl.
"Will you go to soccer practice with Eric again after school?"
Eric is Silas' best friend and they do everything together. Play soccer, build Legos and trade collector cards. Simply everything.
Silas is looking forward to seeing Eric, and technically he would be looking forward to school as well, if he didn't always have to read everything and write it down.

When his classmates or the teacher read a text out loud then Silas has no problem understanding and remembering it.
He has no problem following up.
He is also very good with math as long as it is not written math problems where he has to read first to understand. Those are the worst, along with dictation exercises. Just thinking about it makes Silas feel awful. He got a 'C' again for the last one, and he got lucky on that one too.
He usually gets a 'D'. His hands start sweating as soon as the teacher hands out the work sheets. That is also why his exercise book always looks so messy. And then he gets scolded for not working more neatly.
Silas doesn't even understand why he has so many problems when he is supposed to read something.

Chapter 2

> Today is a good day <

"Silas, come on." His mom is waiting for him
at the door holding his jacket and book bag.
"Are you daydreaming again?" Silas swallows,
grabs his stuff and is off to school.
When he arrives in class, his friends are already
there. Eric, Tom, David and Niclas are trading
Pokemon cards. Silas has them, too.
And he knows almost all of them by heart.
Silas' favorite thing to do is collect things.
He knows the cards with the monsters
especially well.

"Good morning," says Miss Wilson while closing the classroom door. "Who is ready to dive into the wonderful world of numbers?"
Today is a good day. The first class is math, followed by P.E. and finally science. Barely something for him to read or write.
"This is how every day should be like," Silas thinks to himself as he opens his exercise book.

Chapter 3

> Dyslexia or what? <

Silas' mom gets a visit in the afternoon from Eric's mom. They talk about school, and "how they are discussing it on TV. It feels like just yesterday that they were in preschool, but now we already have to think about enrolling them in middle school and if they can qualify for advanced classes." Silas' mom shakes her head. "With his grades in English class Silas will never qualify for advanced classes. I was thinking that maybe he really does have dyslexia." Silas is sick of hearing about this. Lately the only topics seem to be school and grades and grades and school. Sometimes he gets dizzy from hearing the word school all the time. He doesn't even understand himself why reading and writing seems to be so difficult to him. He always tries really hard.

He tries so hard that sometimes he even gets a headache from it. But still his papers are full of bad grades and entries like "Could use improvement" or "You can do better" or "You have to write more neatly" and then there are red marks everywhere from him crossing words out and trying to squeeze in the correct word. Silas often gets really desperate and frustrated. Him and his family have already tried so many different things to help him get better at school, and to make his headaches go away. His movements were monitored, he went to an ear specialist, he went to ergo therapy, and he wears glasses. But nothing has helped him so far. He even took an intelligence test, but his results were not even that bad.

When he was in preschool he knew all types of dinosaurs by heart. He knew if they were carnivores or herbivores, and even what time frames they lived in. Back then he wanted to be an archaeologist, specializing in dinosaurs. But with his grades he can probably forget all about that. "What in the world is wrong with me?" he asks and sadly tiptoes into his room.

Chapter 4

> Dad loses his temper <

Last night Silas' dad has had enough. Again,
Silas failed his dictation exercise, and even got
a bad grade for the upkeep of his notebook.
At first he didn't even want to show it
to mom and dad but he will need
a signature from one of them.
Shucks!
"Alright!" says Dad. "This has to end.
No more soccer for you young man.
From now on you will use the extra time after
school for studying. Starting tomorrow we will
find you a tutor. I have been doing some
research. There is an institute downtown where
you will go three times a week to catch up on
what you didn't get at school."
"Oh no," Silas starts crying.
This means that he will have even less time
for his friends.

School until 4PM and then tutoring until
5.30PM happening three times a week.
And Fridays he already has to go to
ergo therapy. Silas is getting desperate
and angry. And sad. He literally cannot learn
any more. Nothing ever sticks.
He runs into his room, and slams the door.
Mom and dad sadly look at each other.
"But something has to happen," Dad says.
"What will become of him if it continues on like
this?" Mom sits still staring at the table.
"I really don't know," she says quietly
as tears run down her cheeks.

Chapter 5

> At the Learning Institute <

The next morning everything is back to normal. Getting up, breakfast, off to school. But when mom picks him up after class they are not going home directly. "Today," mom explains a little too happy, "we are going to stop by that learning institute that dad was talking about. Maybe it will be just the right thing for you."

"Well perfect," Silas thinks to himself. He actually had plans to stop by at Eric's who wanted to show him his new computer game.

At the learning institute it is not as bad as Silas expected. Everybody is really nice, and he is not the only one there. There are three other children in the group. Plus they have computers that they can use for studying. For English, math and even German they have special classes. As for now Silas will only be tutored in English though. Otherwise, according to dad, it will be too expensive. So from now on Silas will get a tutor three times a week for 90 minutes each. His tutor's name is Justus, and Silas has no problems understanding what Justus is teaching him. The problems only arise when it is Silas' turn to read. That's when the letters simply do what they want. Sometimes they get blurry other times he sees them double or sometimes it even looks like they are jumping up and down.

That's when he cannot focus on the text anymore. It doesn't matter if he wears his glasses or not. Silas then just continues reading how he thinks the word or sentence could have ended. Maybe nobody will notice as long as it still makes sense. But Justus is paying attention and now Silas has to start all over, because again he read something that wasn't even written there. So Silas works even harder what makes his head and eyes start hurting. But that doesn't matter as long as his grades go up. And indeed Silas gets a 'C' in his next dictation exercise. But he still got an 'F' for how his notebook looks.

Chapter 6

> Headaches <

One thing that mom still really worries about are Silas' headaches. So she decides for him to go and see the doctor one more time.
The examination is very thorough, and Silas gets to wear a weird shower cap with snap buttons on it. Then there is a machine that draws a pointy line onto a piece of paper. The doctor says he cannot find anything and sends Silas and his mom off to one of his colleagues, who is a neurologist, a doctor who focuses on brain function. The neurologist continues his tests on Silas. Silas starts believing that they will never ever get to go back home. But even the neurologist cannot find a reason for the headaches, and recommends mom to take Silas to an osteopath. He should see if everything is okay with Silas' cervical vertebra. So Silas and his mom have an appointment there only a couple of days later.
"S. Walter Physiotherapist and Osteopath" it says on the sign.

Again, a very thorough examination is conducted where the doctor looks at Silas' back, his neck, his shoulders, and his legs.

Turns him around, pulls on his feet, feels his head, and pushes down on different areas of his body. One time something cracks but it doesn't hurt. In the end the doctor says that Silas has KISS-Syndrome, and that he has to come back another two or three times. Silas doesn't mind. He kind of feels freshly lubricated. "Just like a robot," he thinks happily. After their visit to the osteopath Silas feels a little better but the letters still get blurry, and his writing gets worse. "Maybe something is wrong with his eyes," Mr. Walter states. But mom says that can't be because they have been to the eye doctor already, and Silas already has glasses. "No, that is not what I mean. Has anybody tested yet if Silas' eyes move the right way?"

Silas just shakes his head. What is that supposed to mean? Of course he can move his eyes. Up and down. Left and right. Works just fine. But the osteopath gives mom a phone number anyway. From an optician who focuses on Functional / Behavioral Optometry. Mom has never heard of that occupation before.

Chapter 7

> The last Try <

Another examination. "This is going to be the last try though," Dad says that evening when they get home. "Now he gets tutored every month then has to go to the osteopath three times, and now I have to spend even more money on his eyes. He already has glasses which weren't cheap either." Silas agrees. He doesn't want to have any more tests done anyway. Or any therapy. But mom keeps pushing dad for it, and then they have an appointment on Tuesday.
"Jenny Wright , Master in Optometry and Functional / Behavioral Optometry,"
is what it says on the sign at the door.
"Holy moly those are really long words," Silas thinks to himself. Good thing he doesn't have to read those out loud. There is another girl in the waiting room who has a bandaid covering one of her eyes.

JENNY RICHTER
- AUGENOPTIKERMEISTERIN -
UND
FUNKTIONALOPTOMETRISTIN

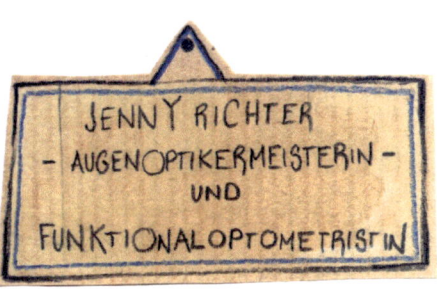

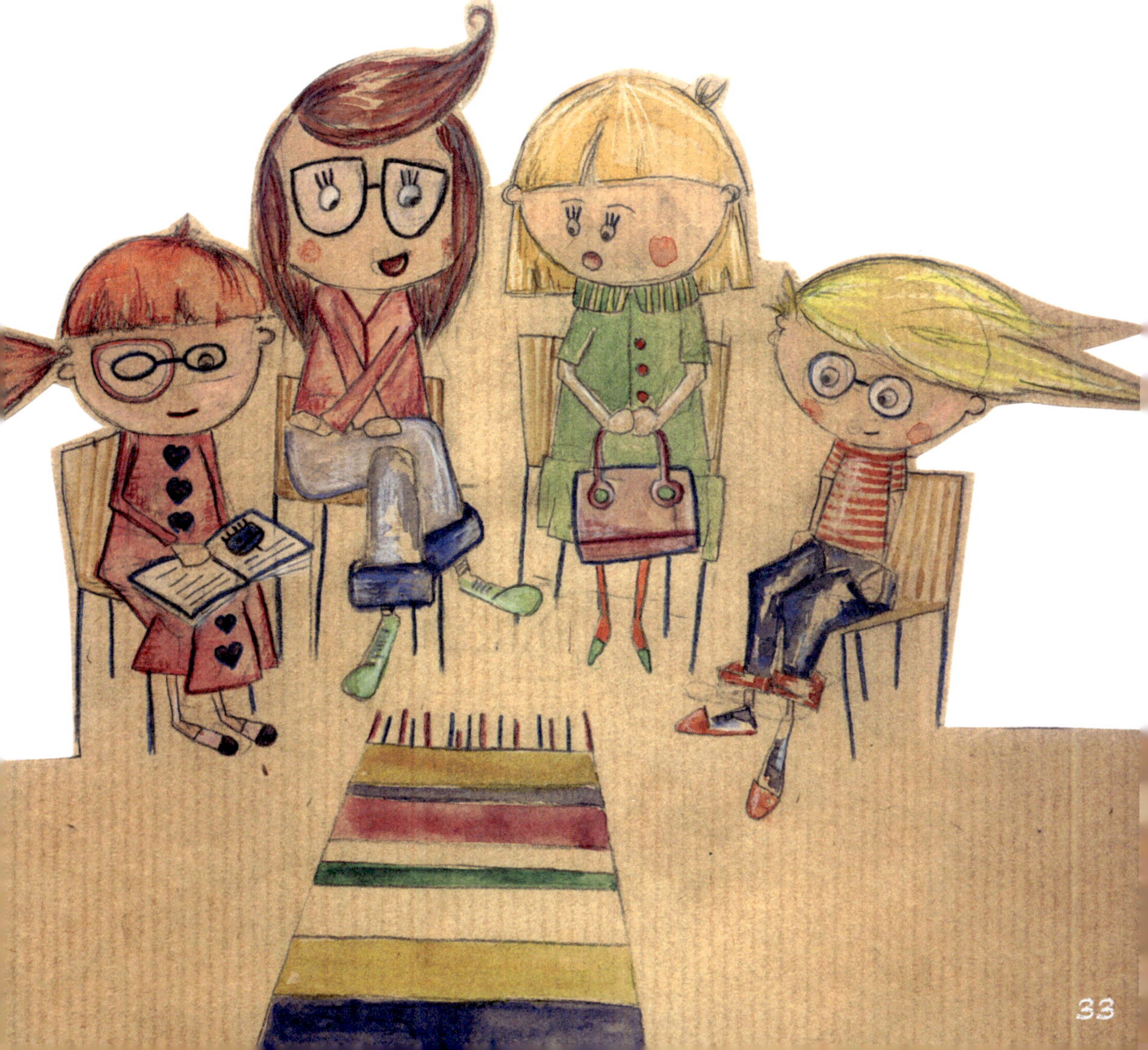

Mom talks to the other girl's mother.
"Sophie is crosseyed"
explains Sophie's mom. "Ms. Wright helps us to wake the lazy eye, and train it to work together with the other eye." The door opens, and a lady shakes Silas' hand. "Hi, I'm Jenny and you must be Silas. Am I right?" Silas and his mom follow the lady over into the other room. That one looks just like a gym. Things are hanging from the ceiling, there are red and black and blueish green tarps hanging at the windows. There are chalk boards with symbols, numbers and letters everywhere. There even is a trampoline in the corner, and balance boards, and a lot of balls. "Reminds me of the ergo therapy place," Silas thinks and sits down at one of the desks. Mom brought some of his homework assignments. Silas feels ashamed because of his grades and his miserable handwriting. But Jenny only takes a quick glance at the papers before returning them to mom. They also had to fill out a questionnaire and Silas was surprised at how many of those symptoms listed there sounded familiar. Headaches, watery and burning eyes, bad handwriting, nausea when riding in the car. Silas wonders how Jenny knows about all this.

Chapter 8

> The Eye Exam <

After going over the questionnaire, and having Silas draw some pictures he now, with only one eye, has to follow a small silver ball that is stuck onto a stick. "Almost like a magic wand," Silas thinks, and tries really hard to concentrate on the ball. But that is not as easy as it sounds. His eye either moves faster than the ball, or the ball gets blurry, and then after just a short amount of time his eye already starts to get watery again.

Now it is the others eye turn. That one is doing a little better. That eye at least doesn't start watering. Jenny has him do the exercise with both eyes together as well, but that is even more difficult. Silas never thought that this would be that much work.

The most difficult thing for him to do is looking at a pen directly in front of his nose followed by one further away. Doing that hurts his eyes, and everything gets blurry. Jenny explains that Silas' eyes don't move in synchronization.

His eyes also have trouble focusing onto the same spot if that spot is really close to his nose.

And his eyes jerk left and right when Silas tries to look at something. Mom checks it out, and now even she can see it. Jenny now grabs a small black machine. "This is a Biopter," she explains. "It helps us to see how your brain processes images that your eyes see."

Silas has to look into the Biopter and draw a star with both hands at the same time. But through the machine everything looks funny, and like it's very far away. When Silas looks at the drawing later, he starts laughing, "that does not look like a star at all." Next thing he has to copy a rectangle. "That's easy. Just copy it," he thinks and starts drawing. But no matter how he holds the pen or twists his head something seems to always be wrong. He either cannot see the tip of his pencil or the rectangle seems to vanish from in front of his eyes. His end result is two rectangles that are half way done.

Chapter 9

> Silas' Eyes are Like Two Horses <

"Well that is okay,"
Jenny says and explains that Silas' eyes are
not working together as a team but against
each other. Just like a stagecoach
with two horses. If the horses don't go the
same speed and in the same direction, then the
stagecoach cannot go straight and one of the
horses might even end up in the ditch.
And that is what Silas experiences when he
has to read something that is one foot
or more away from him. His right eye
is fast enough to read the words
letter by letter, but his left eye drifts off and,
in a matter of speaking, ends up in the ditch.
That is why letters get blurry and make
it hard for Silas to read. Now it is all starting to

make sense to Silas. Jenny also knows why sometimes it takes him longer to read something that is on the chalkboard and other times in his notebook. His ocular lens, the lens in his eye, cannot tighten quick enough to look at something up close. And then it cannot flatten out quick enough to experience something far away. This process takes too long for him. By that time Silas has already used up so much energy trying to make out the words, that he simply just cannot even try to remember what he just read. "Well, now what?" Silas thinks to himself. His mom is also interested in what further steps they can take to make it better. Jenny has an explanation for that as well. There is a visual training that can improve the work of the eye lens as well as the perception. For this, four exercises per day are necessary. "How am I supposed to do that? I cannot come back here every day," Silas protests. "Oh you don't have to," Jenny replies. "I will give you new exercises every two weeks that you can do at home. They will only take you 15-20 minutes every day for a total time of about 8 months. And if you follow the rules and do them every day your eyes should soon learn how to work together as a team." That sounds really good to Silas as well as his mom. Now only dad has to be convinced. That evening the both of them explain to dad what Jenny found out today, and that a vision training is supposed to help Silas from now on. Dad sighs. "And what is the price for that?" Good thing mom knows the answer to that question. "The visual training doesn't cost more than tutoring but there is a timely limit and it will be more effective. Once Silas learns how to control his eyes correctly he will be set for good. It is like riding a bicycle. Once you know how to do it you will never forget." Dad hesitates for a second before agreeing to the plan. And before Silas knows they are on their way over to Jenny's practice again.

Chapter 10

> The Light Shower <

Jenny has to take some measurements before Silas can start with his training. At first he has to look at the bullseye of a target while Jenny flashes colorful dots. Then he gets to sit on a big chair that can move up and down, similar to the one at the eye doctor. Jenny moves little crosses and makes numbers go blurry. Next she uses a green and very bright light to shine into his eye. Silas can see a little star in the middle.

Lastly Silas gets to wear glasses with red lenses and glasses with green lenses, and look through a long pipe and then once again onto the target. "Okay, now it is time for your light shower," Jenny says. "That will make the vision training go a lot easier." Silas has to come back in another week for a control check up.

He can already tell that it is easier for him to see colors. And the world in general seems to be looking more fresh. But then, three weeks later it is finally time for his eye training.

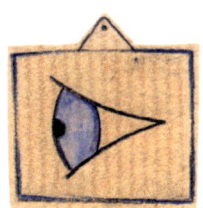

Chapter 11

> Training <

Some exercises are super easy, some are funny, but others are actually pretty difficult, and Silas wouldn't mind dodging those. Mom and Jenny always encourage him to keep going, and as a matter of fact the exercises become easier.
First he always has to do an eye movement exercise. Followed by one for his eye lense so it can learn how to tighten up and flatten out again. Third but not last the ball on a string exercise which is Silas' least favorite.
During this exercise, Silas has to concentrate, with both eyes, on one of three little balls, and the closer the balls are to his face the more difficult it is. The last one is a perception exercise, which is Silas' most favorite one. Sometimes he blindly has to catch a ball, other times draw funny pictures or imagine what they would look like in the mirror.
Dad sometimes joins for that exercise and they get to laugh together.

Chapter 12

> Success! <

By now Silas has visited Jenny six times already, and thanks to mom and dad he has always done his exercises in between the visits. Even though he didn't really feel like doing them sometimes, and rather felt like playing soccer or trying out a new computer game with his friend Luca.

His headaches are slowly getting better which were a big concern of his. His eyes don't get all watery anymore. At least not as easily. He even went to the library last week to borrow a book, and he already made it to page 56. He never thought reading could be this much fun.
Now tutoring is reduced to only once per week, just to work on small mistakes he got wrong due to his vision problem. Silas enjoys school a lot more now. He is not afraid of English class or dictation exercises anymore.
He even got a 'B' last time and the teacher praised the neatness of his notebook.
He has gotten even better in math and in P.E. he is not picked last into a team anymore because even his throwing and catching has improved. Mom and dad are happy that everything seems to go a lot easier and more smoothly than before. And who knows maybe he will soon qualify for advanced classes.

Epilogue:
During the time this book was made Silas kept training his eyes and his vision. On his last certificate from school he only had A's and B's plus a recommendation for advanced classes.

Susanne Nagel is a master optician and optometrist for Functional / Behavioral Optometry and specialized in visual impairment.
After her exam for the master in Optometry in 1992, and the foundation of her own optometry shop, and numerous further training sessions she took the final test to become a Functional / Behavioral Optometrist in 2005. In her book "Silas Learns How to Read" she draws attention to the problems of children who have a visual disruption. Children struggle every day because not enough attention is being paid towards the function of the eyes.

Susanne Nagel lives in Germany with her husband and their four kids.

notes